**Community Care
Practice Handbooks**

General Editor: Martin Davies

Rights and Responsibilities

Discussion of Moral Dimensions
in Social Work

Community Care Practice Handbooks

General Editor: Martin Davies

Rights and Responsibilities

Discussion of Moral Dimensions in Social Work

Neil Leighton
Richard Stalley
David Watson

HEINEMANN EDUCATIONAL BOOKS
LONDON

Heinemann Educational Books Ltd
22 Bedford Square, London WC1B 3HH
LONDON   EDINBURGH   MELBOURNE   AUCKLAND
HONG KONG   SINGAPORE   KUALA LUMPUR   NEW DELHI
IBADAN   NAIROBI   JOHANNESBURG
EXETER (NH)   KINGSTON   PORT OF SPAIN

British Library Cataloguing in Publication Data

Leighton, Neil
  Rights and responsibilities: discussion of moral
  dimensions in social work.—(Community care
  practice handbooks; 11)
  1. Social service—Great Britain—Case Studies
  I. Title   II. Stalley, Richard F.   III. Watson,
  David   IV. Series
  361.3'2'0941   HV245

  ISBN 0-435-82515-1

Printed in Great Britain by Biddles Ltd, Guildford, Surrey

Contents

Acknowledgements

Our interest in the use of case studies to introduce social work students and social workers to philosophical discussion of values began with participation in the CCETSW Workshop on their discussion paper 13, 'Values in Social Work', held at Wolfson Hall, Glasgow University, 24–25 March 1977. Participation in further workshops on this theme, in Manchester and elsewhere, and our use of this kind of material in teaching, has demonstrated its suitability for the task in hand. Our thanks go to all who have joined in the discussions we set up, and in particular to Miss J. H. Grant, Mr J. S. Scott and Neil Leighton, whose case studies from the Glasgow Workshop we have used here. The other case studies come from 'The position and task of the staff supervisor in a local authority social services department', a DHSS report (l.d.s. 6685/1(I)EL), and we thank Ken Corcoran for his permission to reproduce material from that report. All the case studies used here have been edited with a view to their use as teaching material and responsibility for their final form lies with us.

We should particularly like to thank four other people: Donald Houston, for advice on the use of case studies in teaching and introducing the material, and Anne Valentine and Wilma White, in Glasgow, and Kathleen Brookes, in Bristol, for use of their typing skills.

Introduction

In this small book we aim to provide means by which social work students and social workers can examine the content and influence of values in their own working lives. In Part I we offer a range of brief case studies grouped around a number of important themes. Each group of case studies is preceded by an introduction to the theme and followed by a note on useful reading material. Each individual case study is followed by comment directing discussion towards the theme as it arises in the particular case. In Part II we add notes on a number of terms that recur in the case studies and comments, introducing you to at least some of their philosophical complexities.

Our central purpose in presenting these case studies is to draw your attention towards a particular, and we think fundamentally important, interpretation of the familiar comment that 'the *personal* dimension is everywhere in social work'. The social worker's clients present him* with all manner of facets of the *human* condition, and he in his turn must strive to hold on to and to convey his humanity. There are, of course, rival views about what it is to be human, where to be human is to be not just a member of our species but to live in a certain, recommended way. However, central to the human condition as *we* recognise and recommend it is an understanding of oneself as related to others by a network of commitments. As *people* both client and social worker live in a world in which they inherit, adopt, negotiate and abandon commitments in a range of social identities, as sons and daughters, fathers and mothers, friends, person helped and person helping, people co-operating. This network of commitments structures our expectations of ourselves and others, gives us purpose and reasons to act. For each individual, one might suggest, his own network of commitments makes up what might be called his moral identity, so that moral integrity would be understood as relative to a person's fulfilling or not fulfilling the commitments making up that identity.

* Those who want to take issue with our use of 'he' etc., and who have an interest in philosophical issues, should enjoy Janet Radcliffe Richards' *The Sceptical Feminist*, Routledge & Kegan Paul, 1980.

The commitments we undertake express value-judgements about how we desire to stand in relation to others. In discussing the commitments undertaken by a client to, say, members of his family, or his social worker, or by a social worker to his client, social workers make, explore and encourage value-judgements. The social work practitioner must study and practise discussion of his own values and the values of others if he is to act in a personal, self-conscious and purposeful way. Competence in the art of working with values is competence in an art which he will practise for the length of his working days.

We have thought it desirable to supply the theme introductions and case comments because it is often difficult to relate problems encountered in practice to the more abstract theoretical discussions found in textbooks of philosophy, or of any other discipline for that matter. The disadvantage is that our comments may bias readers towards one interpretation of the case studies when other interpretations might be quite justifiable and equally fruitful for discussion. In using this material in teaching we have often found that participants have noticed points we have missed or have suggested interpretations which we had not considered. So it is important to emphasise that although our comments, and indeed the listed reading, suggest particular ways of approaching the case studies, other approaches may have just as much or even more to be said for them. Our aim has been simply to provide a framework within which the reader can explore and develop his skills in the art of working with values, whether as a member of a self-help or tutor-led group or working by himself. We have chosen themes of recurring importance to social workers and you will probably be able to find material relating to these themes among case histories to which you have access. They may well cast a different light on those themes from that cast by the studies we have chosen. Further, our framework provides a model for discussion of themes that you regard as important but which are here omitted. Begin to create your own material.

You will almost certainly not be familiar with the *form* of philosophical discussion of values. Indeed, philosophers themselves argue about what form such discussion must take. Some philosophers say that when we make a value-judgement we should reach it as the conclusion of a sound *argument* in which some crucial reference is made to facts. And yet it seems that sometimes two people may refer to the same fact in support of incompatible value-judgements. Others, again, say that value-judgements express emotions or attitudes. But then it seems there can be no genuine moral disagreement, only emotional or attitudinal discord. And there are other contested views.

However, *we* draw a distinction between moralising and philosophical discussion of moral value-judgements. In moralising we make moral judgements, we say what people ought or ought not to do, or direct them to do what we think they ought to do. In philosophical discussion we are, rather, concerned, amongst other things, first to *understand* the value-judgement made and, second, *to discover the grounds* of that value-judgement, if any. The first task may require us to engage in discussion aimed at clarification of the value-judgement, the second leads to critical evaluation of the logical relation between grounds offered and the judgement made. Few social workers see their task as that of moralising. Thank goodness. And yet social workers often properly and usefully participate in discussions about what people ought to do. In our view a necessary though not a sufficient condition of skilful participation in such discussions is practice in philosophical discussion of value-judgements, of the kind outlined. The case studies invite your participation in discussion of this kind.

If you would like to see further philosophical discussion of the nature of value-judgements, you might look at any one of the following: Hospers (1962), Frankena (1963), Raphael (1970), or Warnock (1967). For discussion of other areas of philosophical debate and of criteria for good argument in general, see Lindley, Fellows and Macdonald (1978) and Hanfling (1978).

Perhaps we may conclude with a health warning. Precisely because the experience of valuing touches upon our moral identity and our humanity, our engagement in discussions of these themes can be a painful encounter. The pain can be eased by focusing primarily upon the values of the inhabitants of the case studies, but this should not be sustained. Of course social workers are concerned to help clients judge what they ought to do, but social workers themselves must make value-judgements about what they, social workers, ought to do in a particular case. Such moral questions are particularly acute in cases in which the worker has moral objections to the client's actions or decisions, or, perhaps as common, in cases in which the worker has moral objections to his employer's views of what ought to be done, or, rather, cut and left undone. You will find use of these case-studies to be of personal significance only when your discussions include consideration of your own value-judgements. Again, discussion of how one's own values affect ways of working in particular cases may be delayed by demands for more information. In most of the cases here presented, more information might have been usefully given. You should feel free to add detail. But then you should go on to discuss its moral significance in the particular case, for this leads into discussion of such values. The question always remains: given such facts, what ought you to do?

PART I

Case Studies

1 Responsibility and Reciprocity

Introduction

As Robert Pinker has observed, social services reflect our dispositions both to remember and to forget our social obligations (1971, p. 135). Our ideas about our obligations to others play a large part in the social policies we develop, the ways in which they are implemented, and above all play a large part in determining the kind of social relations we have with those other people as fellow citizens and as social service workers.

As members of society we all have rights and obligations. Some of these are shared by all members of society, but there are other rights and obligations that arise out of the particular roles or 'social identities' which we have. For example, there is a particular social relation between people whose 'social identities' are, respectively, 'doctor' and 'patient'. And each identity carries with it certain rights and obligations. The doctor has an obligation, amongst others, to use his skills to promote the health of his patient, and a right, amongst others, to all relevant information. Our obligations, particularly those that arise from a special role or social identity, are often called our 'responsibilities'. We may, for example, talk about the responsibilities of doctor and patient instead of talking about their obligations. Someone who takes his responsibilities seriously and does his best to fulfil them can be said to behave responsibly or to be a responsible sort of person. Conversely to be irresponsible is to neglect one's responsibilities. Not that the rights and responsibilities attached to social identities are beyond debate.

The cases in this section are all ones in which some might say that the client was failing in his responsibilities to society or to those about him, and in which we may also say that society has failed in its responsibilities towards the people who have become clients. In some cases the social services themselves seem to be involved in this 'forgetfulness' of society's responsibilities. If we do think that society has failed in its responsibilities to some individuals then the question arises 'How should we react if these individuals then fail in *their* responsibilities towards society?' Is it *just* to penalise them for failing to do their part when the community has not done its part? Should we think in terms of compensation or of reverse discrimination?

There is another sense of 'responsibility' in which we talk of a person being responsible for something which has happened or bearing responsibility for it and mean thereby that he is liable to punishment or reward, praise or blame for it. We are usually held responsible and thus liable to punishment for illegal actions except in cases where we acted under some kind of compulsion or did not know what we were doing. Special difficulties arise, however, when delinquent actions can apparently be traced back to bad social conditions. People have become increasingly unhappy about holding those who commit delinquent acts in such circumstances responsible for what they do. If we do not hold them responsible, and therefore do not punish them, what should we do? If we simply ignore such behaviour, will there not be an injustice done to the victims?

These difficulties grow more severe if we accept a version of the philosophical theory of determinism according to which all human behaviour is ultimately caused by events outside the person himself. Some people believe that if determinism is true no one can ever be responsible for his acts, and all traditional ideas of responsibility and punishment collapse. Part 3 of the reading list at the end of this chapter gives access to useful philosophical discussion of this problem.

Such problems may not seem to concern social workers directly because, it will be said, it is not the job of a social worker to administer punishment. But they do concern him indirectly because, as society has become reluctant to punish offenders, it has increasingly looked to social workers to *treat* them. And treatment cannot begin without some view about the explanation of the difficulty to be treated. What is appropriate treatment often depends directly upon our view of the client's capacity to behave responsibly, or his responsibility for some behaviour which provides the occasion for contact, such as an offence. Any challenge to the view that clients can be responsible in both these ways is of *direct* concern.

Case One: Roy
Roy is the youngest member of an immigrant family known to the Social Services for many years. The husband, now 53, has chronic tuberculosis and has had a lung removed. There are five girls now aged 14, 13, 12, 11, 10, and then Roy, 9.

Over the years help has been centred on the truanting of one of the girls and the family's poverty. The father cannot always work, and when he does he earns low wages. Otherwise the family exists on supplementary benefit with direct payment of rent etc. They are chronically in debt to all the usual services, HP, etc. They live on a run-down council estate where 'problem families' are housed.

Roy has recently and uncharacteristically begun to be physically violent to other children and elderly people. School, police, and other children's parents have put great pressure on the Social Services Department to 'put him away'. It seems that Roy is well behaved in the classroom and at home, but once outside with his 'gang' he outdoes them all.

Comment

We might use this case to consider the social relations between Roy and his family and others in the wider community, and to consider our social obligations to each other as members of society.

The case notes make it clear that a number of social services have been used by this family, from hospital treatment to direct payment of rent. In these ways others seem to have acknowledged and at least partly fulfilled what they see as their social obligations to Roy and his family. On the other hand, some social obligations may have been forgotten. Can you identify *disservices* the family has suffered? To whose benefit? Can social services be also thought of as compensation for such disservices? Is that compensation adequate?

Further, Roy himself is harming others by his present behaviour. Do past disservices suffered by him and his family, or any other feature of Roy's 'social background' lessen his responsibility for his present behaviour? Is the fact that his violence is 'uncharacteristic' important? Should our view of his degree of responsibility affect our work with him? In this case, and in those which follow, consider whether any degree of client responsibility, for any behaviour, would preclude others' responsibility to aid him.

Case Two: Rose

Rose is the third child of four, living with their mother, who is separated from her husband. The family have been known for four years, since the mother was imprisoned for shoplifting. The eldest child, then 16, was put on probation for the same offence and looked after the younger ones while her mother was in prison.

Since then Rose, who has impaired hearing, has been in trouble, stealing and truanting. She spent a profitless time in a children's home under a care order. She continues to steal and does not work; a supervision order continues. Now at 18, she faces prosecution for stealing as an adult. Concern is growing about the behaviour of the youngest child, the only boy.

Comment

In many ways Rose's problems seem like Roy's. Both are behaving in ways which are harmful to others and in both cases the misbehaviour seems to be related in some way to unfortunate home circumstances. But there are some differences between the two cases which may be significant. Rose's delinquency seems characteristic of her whereas Roy's was not. Rose's problems began when her mother was sent to prison which suggests that they may have been caused directly by the intervention of official agencies. Rose has already had a period in a children's home whereas this treatment is only under consideration for Roy. In both cases the questions to be answered seem to be much the same. The young people are needing to acquire more responsible ways of behaving if they and those around them are to have a satisfactory life. The main difficulty is to see how this can be brought about. In both cases one may feel unhappy about attributing responsibility for the misbehaviour to the young people themselves because it seems to be due to external causes. How should this affect our attitude towards them and our work with them? Could it be said that they deserve some kind of compensation for the disadvantages they have suffered? What useful form could such compensation take? If they have a right to have emotional needs met, how can such compensation be 'paid' to them? Can it be purchased for them? Can it be bought in the market place or is it essentially a voluntary commitment? Or must it, in practice, be a mixture of both elements?

Case Three: Mrs P and Bruce

The P family has been known to the agency for 15 years. Mrs P (now aged 69) has been in psychiatric hospital 20 times over this period. She is treated with drugs for paraphrenia. She is well known and feared in the locality, given to attacking people who feature in her aural hallucinations. She has been charged with assault many times, and usually fined. Whenever she is in hospital her behaviour presents no difficulty, so she is soon discharged to out-patient care again. The Social Services Department receives constant complaints from the public, though these are tapering off as her condition slowly abates with increasing physical frailty.

Her place in the locality's attention is being taken by Bruce, her 32-year-old son. When he was 26 Bruce emigrated to Canada, but began to develop symptoms of schizophrenia and returned. Since then he too has been attacking local people and their property, apparently without provocation. Like his mother, his behaviour in hospital is easily manageable, so he is soon discharged to have his drugs supervised as an out-patient. With great difficulty he was helped into a job he could manage, but was made redundant within a year.

Bruce's condition is now less easy to handle. He used to admit his delusions and accept his need for help. He now claims to be perfectly all right; his hospital admissions are less easy to engineer and he leaves as he wishes.

Concern and anger in the locality is such that social workers are inevitably involved in advising abused people of their rights. A recent private summons of Bruce for damage to property has precipitated a new opportunity to review the situation. The court accepted advice to make residence in hospital a condition of a probation order.

Mr P senior, also 69, is not well, and has obviously had a most difficult life with his wife and son. There is a married daughter who sees him, but not Mrs P or Bruce.

Comment

Like Roy and Rose Mrs P and Bruce are behaving in anti-social ways although there are reasons for supposing that they are not fully responsible for what they do. But Mrs P and Bruce seem to be suffering from definite mental disorders so in their case it is not simply a matter of a poor home environment. It therefore seems much less likely that they could be helped by social work techniques. If there is any hope for them it seems to lie in the application of medical techniques such as drug therapy. The problem remains 'what attitude should society in general and social workers in particular adopt towards them?' One possibility would be compulsory medical treatment but this raises grave ethical problems particularly now that Bruce no longer admits that he is deluded. What right do we have to coerce people against their will to be manipulated by the use of drugs or other medical means? What grounds, if any, would justify us in doing this? If we press the point even harder we might ask whether we are really justified in saying that Bruce's view of the world is a deluded one? If voluntary medical treatment is not accepted and compulsory treatment is excluded on ethical grounds then we are left with the problem of dealing with Bruce's anti-social behaviour. We could use the criminal law but this may seem quite inappropriate for someone who is mentally ill. Indeed, it looks as though in Bruce's case it has simply been used as a technique for securing compulsory medical treatment. If Bruce does not see himself as mentally ill, should the use of the criminal law cease to be perceived as 'inappropriate' by us? Is it only *our* word for how we experience it, in the same way as 'mental illness' may be *our* word for Bruce's perception of the world?

Reading

1. On the ideas of social identity and social obligations:
   Downie (1971);
   Feinberg (1973).

2. On social obligations arising from disservices, and the idea of compensatory provision:
   Titmuss (1968), Chs. 11 and 13;
   Glennerster and Hatch (1974).

3. On responsibility for our behaviour:
   Langford (1972), Ch. 1;
   Peters (1958), Chs. 1 and 6;
   O'Connor (1972);
   Foren and Bailey (1968).

4. For further reading see the Notes in Part II on Punishment, Responsibility, Rights, Role or Social Identity, Self-determination, and Social Justice.

2 Self-determination and the Right to Intervene

Introduction

The principle of client self-determination is often regarded as one of the basic principles of social work. This principle, as it is usually interpreted, requires a social worker not to try to control his client's behaviour or to take his decisions for him. So the social worker must not exercise any kind of dominating or controlling influence over his clients; he must not use coercive methods or even strong persuasion. Of course even the most enthusiastic advocates of self-determination admit that there may be cases where the social worker has to take the decision out of the client's hands but there is difficulty in saying precisely what the limits of self-determination are. Problems of this kind are raised by the cases of Anne and Mrs MacL. In both cases the social worker has seriously to consider taking decisions on behalf of the client rather than leaving the client to make up her own mind.

Closely related to problems of self-determination are problems about privacy. Social workers often become aware of people who seem to need help but who are unwilling to discuss their problems with a social worker. Here there is no question of controlling the client's decisions but it may seem that a social worker who insisted on intervening would be infringing the client's right to privacy. This seems to be at least part of the problem in the case of Mr Larkin.

In discussing these questions it may be helpful to relate them to philosophical discussions of liberty. The most celebrated writer on this topic is John Stuart Mill. Mill's essay *On Liberty* is a passionate defence of the right to individual freedom. Mill insists that the state or society at large may only interfere with the liberty of the individual to prevent him from doing harm to others. So, in Mill's view, it would be wrong to coerce a person in any way simply to prevent him harming himself or to prevent him doing something which is deemed to be morally wrong but does not harm others. But Mill does allow that his principles do not apply to children or to others who are incapable of taking rational decisions.

A social worker who had read Mill might well suggest that there are two kinds of limit on the rights of a client to self-determination: the social worker may interfere with the client's freedom either when he is in danger of harming others or when he is incapable of taking a rational decision. In practice many social workers would probably agree with this, but it by no means solves all the problems. A large number of clients are in situations where they might be said to be incapable of taking rational decisions because they are subject to social or emotional pressures or mental illness. In many cases there is also the possibility that what the client does will affect others. So, if social workers felt themselves entitled to interfere with a client's freedom *whenever they* judged that the client was incapable of acting rationally or was in danger of harming others, the way would be open to a very authoritarian style of social work, with quite extensive interference in clients' lives. Thus it cannot be in every case where the client may be deemed irrational or likely to harm others that the social worker has the right to intervene, but only in some relatively extreme cases. The difficulty is in deciding what circumstances justify intervention in any particular case.

In discussing these problems it is important to distinguish between questions about whether the social worker has the moral right to intervene and about whether it would be useful for the social worker to intervene. In the cases of Anne and Mr Larkin, for example, one of the points to be considered is whether social work intervention may sometimes be counter-productive.

Case One: Mrs MacL

Mrs MacL is a widow of 82 years, living in a ground floor one-bedroomed flat, one of four in a block situated in an area populated predominantly by middle-aged and elderly people.

Mr MacL died some 20 years ago. The only relatives Mrs MacL has are now old and live at a considerable distance, so that contact is almost non-existent. Mrs MacL has a few friends who take her out for trips in the car and visit her at home but on the whole her social contacts are limited. She is almost totally deaf even with a hearing aid, and although she is fairly mobile within the home she has the services of a home help for one hour a day.

This case was referred to the Social Work Department by a neighbour living above Mrs MacL's flat. The neighbour had smelled gas and had asked the Gas Board to disconnect Mrs MacL's supply. The Gas Board visited but could find no fault with

Mrs MacL's gas appliance, a cooker. They could not disconnect her supply and decided to take no further action. This situation was causing considerable anxiety especially among the other elderly occupants of the block, most of whom are clients of the Department. There had recently been a gas explosion in the town which had totally destroyed a house, causing many injuries. This was still very fresh in their minds and they were understandably concerned for their homes and their own safety.

A male social worker visited Mrs MacL only to find her alone. He was unable to hold a conversation with her because of her lack of hearing and so decided to return when the home help, who had also reported smelling gas, would be present.

At the second interview the social worker wrote notes to Mrs MacL and she gave verbal replies. It was suggested that a small electric cooker could prove more suitable for her needs and that the DHSS could be asked for financial assistance. A visit was made by the DHSS but they informed the Social Work Department that they could not give financial aid as Mrs MacL had sufficient funds in the bank to meet the outlay for a new cooker.

The social worker visited Mrs MacL again and informed her of the DHSS decision. The new cooker would cost £60. This was not acceptable to Mrs MacL as she saw no need for a new cooker when her existing model had been viewed by the Gas Board as being in good working order. The social worker then attempted to make clear that Mrs MacL, because of lapses in concentration, was forgetting to switch off the gas after cooking her meal and that the neighbours had reported smelling gas. The dangers of such a practice were made clear to Mrs MacL but she was unprepared to accept this and stood by her decision to keep her existing cooker. The degree of danger could not be assessed as no one knew whether Mrs MacL *always* forgot to switch off the cooker or whether this happened only occasionally.

Comment

One initial difficulty about this case is that it is not entirely clear how real the danger of a gas explosion is. Has the social worker perhaps been too hasty in accepting the neighbours' view that there is such a danger?

Assuming that the danger is a real one, the case raises substantial problems about self-determination. Some social workers may be inclined to adopt a very directive approach either on the grounds that the old lady is incapable of taking a rational decision or on the grounds that she is a danger to her neighbours. Others may say that to put pressure on the old lady in this way would be an unjustifiable infringement of her self-determination. Do you think it would be right to use coercive or directive methods in such a case? If so, on what grounds?

Even if it is agreed that someone ought to ensure that Mrs MacL changes her method of cooking it is not clear that the social worker is the person who should enforce such a requirement. Perhaps it should really be the function of some other agency such as the Gas Board. Do you think that social workers are the right people to intervene in such cases? Or have they been too willing to shoulder responsibilities that should not really be theirs?

Case Two: Mr Larkin

Mr Larkin, who is a bank manager, referred his marital problem to a marriage counsellor. His wife, he said, was going through the change of life and was being very difficult in her attitude towards him. He could do nothing right in her eyes and she did not speak to him but wrote messages. Sometimes when she mislaid something she imagined that her husband had taken it. She then stole some of his possessions in retaliation. She had drawn the children into the conflict: the 12-year-old boy would not speak to his father, the 9-year-old girl still spoke to him but was under pressure from her mother not to – sometimes her father met her at school to have a proper talk with her. Mr Larkin asked whether the counsellor could visit the home and speak with his wife. His wife was not prepared to seek help from a counsellor or psychiatrist. Mr Larkin seemed most upset at the gulf appearing between him and the children. The marriage has had few emotional rewards for him for a long while.

The counsellor took the view that as there was no indication from the wife or children that they wanted help in changing the situation then it would be unwarranted interference to invade their privacy. Because there appeared to be no joint commitment to any 'treatment' of the marital and family situation then it was to be presumed that there was no prospect of a positive response to the intervention.

Three weeks later the 12-year-old Ronald was before the Juvenile Court for stealing and the Court learned that he had also been missing school. A social worker then visited the family to make a social enquiry for the Court and discovered that the home was a battleground between the parents. He formed the view that

Ronald was reacting to his stressful home situation and made it clear to the parents that if Ronald was to improve his social performance then it was necessary for there to be a reduction of the stress. He put it to the parents that since they were both concerned to overcome their son's problems they would have to work out some joint plan for reducing the expressed tensions between them; the social worker would help them in promoting the plan.

Comment
The most striking point about this case is the contrast between the approach of the marriage counsellor, who withdrew as soon as he discovered that Mrs Larkin was unwilling to change, and that of the local authority social worker, who was prepared to be much more assertive.

One explanation of the difference between the approaches adopted by the two workers might be that they differed in their theoretical or ethical presuppositions. For example, the counsellor's approach may have been determined by a psychotherapeutic view; he may have believed that nothing could be achieved without the willing participation of Mrs Larkin. Or he may have believed that further involvement would have been an unjustifiable infringement of Mrs Larkin's right to privacy.

Another explanation of the differing approach of the two workers might be that the marriage counsellor was involved only at the request of Mr Larkin whereas the local authority worker became involved on the instructions of a court after the son's delinquent behaviour had come to light. Although the boy's misbehaviour was apparently an overt expression of the anguish which had been present in the home all along it might be argued that law breaking justifies interference with the privacy of the family whereas mere suffering does not. Do you think that the son's delinquency does make an important difference to the situation?

This case also raises questions about the responsibilities and duties of parents towards their children. There is more about these problems in Chapter 3. In this case, for example, should Mrs Larkin willingly sacrifice her privacy for the sake of her son, even if she accepts the alleged relation between his behaviour and her current attitudes?

Case Three: Anne and baby Sandra
Anne and Jack married when she was 17 and he was 20. A year later Sandra was born, and from the beginning the baby seemed

miserable. She was in and out of hospital for 'failure to thrive' and Anne's awkwardness with her led to the paediatrician involving the Social Services Department, as well as the health visitor, in the baby's supervision.

The GP's opinion was that Anne had never had a satisfactory relationship with her mother. Although not technically handicapped, Anne did very poorly at school. She rarely sees her own relatives, but Jack's family take a very active interest in them and the baby.

The social worker and health visitor each visited several times weekly. During periods when Sandra was in hospital Anne visited her daily, but she never seemed able to handle and feed the baby, even with the help of hospital staff. A care order was considered: Anne was prepared to let Sandra be in hospital, but not to let her go into local authority care. The paediatrician thought she might not survive at home.

When Sandra was 8 months old she was diagnosed as having coeliac disease, which would account for her rejection of food and general failure to thrive. A special diet resulted in immediate improvement. Sandra may have to continue on this diet for many years. Hospital staff also found Sandra easier to feed now. At a case conference the social worker reported that Jack has beaten Anne once, though Anne described it as an accident. The health visitor reported that when Sandra was at home Anne had got into the habit of taking her almost daily to the clinic to be weighed; if she saw any health visitor in the street she would speak to her, even across the road, insisting 'I *have* fed her.' Concern was expressed by the health visitor at the possibility of 'service-generated anxiety'. It was also observed that Anne overdressed Sandra, causing her discomfort, and played with her as if she were a doll.

Comment

So far as one can judge from the case report the involvement of the social workers in this case was prompted, in part at least, by the assumption that the baby's failure to thrive resulted from the inadequacy of her mother's care. This assumption proved mistaken but the involvement of social workers in the case continued. It looks as though this involvement did harm by creating an attitude of dependence in the client and generating unnecessary anxiety.

In this particular case you may want to consider whether social work intervention was justified in the period before coeliac disease was diagnosed and if so what form it should have taken, and whether continuing social work intervention was justified after the diagnosis of the disease. But the case also raises wider issues that concern social work generally. Social work intervention is always based on a judgement of the situation. The social worker believes there is a problem which can be helped by social work methods and he usually has some idea what the problem is. But there is always a possibility that this judgement is mistaken. Indeed a radical critic of social work might complain that contemporary social work frequently involves the imposition of the social worker's incomplete and partial view of the situation on the client who is really the one who knows it best. It might also be alleged that social work often does create the kind of dependent and anxious attitude which seems to have been caused in Anne's case. If this is so, it may inhibit the growth of responsible attitudes and the self-fulfilment of the client instead of helping them. How would you reply to these charges? Is there any way in which social work practice can avoid these alleged dangers in this case and in general?

Reading
1. On self-determination:
   McDermott (1975).

2. On the right to intervene:
   Watson (1975);
   Wootton (1960);
   Foren and Bailey (1968).

3. For further reading see the Notes in Part II on Liberty, Mental Health and Mental Illness, Moral Harm, Rights, and Self-determination.

3 Anti-social Clients

Introduction

The cases in this chapter concern clients whose behaviour might be categorised as irresponsible or anti-social. Their problems arise because they are unwilling or unable to live up to the standards expected by their neighbours or by society at large. They become the clients of social workers, not because they feel themselves to be in distress, but because other people or other agencies find their conduct intolerable and expect social workers to effect some kind of reform. In talking about such cases it is practically impossible to avoid making value-judgements about the clients' behaviour for the reason that their 'problem' is simply a failure to accept or live up to a set of values which other people find acceptable. The social worker may feel a conflict among three or four sets of values – his own, those of the client and those of the agency or society at large. This is particularly evident in the case of Mrs Walsh. Other people expect children to be clean and well disciplined, Mrs Walsh seems to value an 'irresponsible generosity'; the social worker who compiled the report obviously feels some sympathy with both views.

Some people might think that it is not the business of the social worker to make value-judgements about what his client does or to attempt to change the client's values. They might feel that it was wrong to try to make clients conform to society's norms. But the values of society in cases like these are not arbitrary. If clients such as John Carter, the Stephens and Mrs Walsh do persist in their behaviour, real distress is likely to result either to themselves or to their children or to other people. If the social worker is to prevent this distress he will have to bring about some kind of change in his client's behaviour. So a social worker cannot simply ignore questions of values where they are linked to suffering.

The traditional way of dealing with those who behave in an anti-social way was to use punishment or other kinds of coercion. In all the cases in this section at least some consideration was given to using such methods. But social workers have regarded coercion as being incompatible with their own approach. Their aim has been to help the client to change for himself, but there are obvious difficulties where the client is either unwilling or unable to change. Without the co-operation of the client the social worker can do little, so society then has to decide whether to use coercive methods or simply put up with the anti-social behaviour.

Even when the client appears co-operative there is a danger that the social worker's 'helping' approach may lend itself to manipulation by the client. If he emphasises his imagined or real personal difficulties the client may be able to play on the social worker's sympathy and to use the social worker as a means of avoiding the unpleasant consequences of his own acts. In all three cases in this section this kind of danger may be present, and it is at least possible that if the clients were simply left to face things for themselves they might be able to improve their own behaviour.

It is sometimes tempting to regard all anti-social behaviour as though it were a kind of disease. One might, for example, regard John Carter as being in some way mentally sick. The trouble is that anti-social behaviour is not like an ordinary illness: it is not painful in itself and in itself it does not normally cause the death of the person who behaves in an anti-social fashion. If we treat anti-social behaviour as though it were a disease we will be treating it as though it were bad for the agent whereas it is not usually bad for him in itself but for other people. If we treat anti-social behaviour as a disease we may be disguising what is really a moral judgement and dressing it up as though it were a kind of judgement of medical fact. So there is a danger that we may pretend that we are helping a person by curing a disease which he has when in fact we are manipulating him to fit in with the values of others. For this reason some influential modern writers have been very suspicious of the whole concept of a mental disease. Whether or not we go this far we should be clear that we cannot avoid the kinds of moral judgement involved in cases like the ones in this chapter simply by saying that the client is 'sick' and needs 'treatment'.

Case One: John Carter

John Carter, a tall, fine-featured man of 27 appeared in court charged with stealing a car and was remanded in prison for probation reports. Whilst in custody he made a suicidal gesture, attempting to hang himself. Carter had been on probation before and the probation officer therefore contacted the officer who had supervised him at that time. The latter described Carter as 'a pathological liar' and 'a complete waste of time'; he was unable to form relationships of any integrity and there was therefore no foundation for casework.

When interviewed, Carter talked easily about his origins and his past; he was obviously intelligent and highly articulate and knew the language of psychiatry. His father was a headmaster; his mother was a student nurse. His paternity was concealed and he was brought up by his father's mother. His father died when he was ten and his grandmother died when he was twelve. He was then moved around among relatives but recalls no one of any significance. He entered the Army as soon as he was old enough, was discharged on medical grounds but later re-enlisted and managed to conceal his past for more than a year. During this period he married, but the marriage was not successful. He claims that he is unable to maintain responsible relationships. He sees himself as having not received love and affection, his birth a source of disgrace to his father; the only people he loved died when he was young. He argues that he cannot be expected to show care and affection or responsible conduct because of his bitter experience of the world. He gets a real feeling of achievement from defeating the complex rules or society: re-enlistment in the Army, stowing away and getting into America and even obtaining a work permit in the USA were landmarks for him. He claimed to have a pilot's licence and a small private income from his father's estate. He was undoubtedly attractive and had a constant stream of girls whom he involved in trying to help him. When the relationships became demanding upon him he would ask the probation officer to try to acquaint the girls with the facts of his inability to be anything other than a recipient of a relationship, and how damaging he could be to them. He talked easily and unashamedly to his probation officer and much of what he said could be verified but he missed out important truths and it seems he will continue to commit offences or to defraud people emotionally if not to their financial detriment.

Comment

The fundamental question here is whether John Carter should simply be treated as an incorrigible rogue who can be controlled, if at all, only by the threat of punishment or whether he should be regarded as somebody who is really mentally ill or emotionally disturbed and who therefore deserves sympathetic treatment. If it is a case for punishment, then social work involvement would seem inappropriate. On the other hand there are real difficulties in regarding people like this as ill or disturbed. Isn't the main thing wrong with him that he has failed to live up to acceptable moral standards? If we regard this as grounds for saying that he is ill, are we not simply dressing up our moral judgements in a medical disguise? Or are there perhaps other grounds besides his immoral behaviour which might justify us in saying that he is ill? In any case it's difficult to see how one could regard John's behaviour as a problem unless one took for granted a certain set of moral standards. This raises the question whether it is right, or even possible, to adopt a non-judgemental approach in dealing with such cases.

Case Two: the Stephens Family

Mr and Mrs Stephens have five children living with them, four of Mrs Stephen's previous marriage and one of this marriage. Three of them are teenagers who have made themselves unpopular on the council estate where they live because of their undisciplined and destructive behaviour. Mr Stephens has had an irregular work pattern and an industrial injury causes recurrent medical problems. He is also inclined to bouts of heavy drinking. Mrs Stephens often says that she is fed up with his behaviour, particularly the drinking and violence which comes with it, and that she would like to divorce him. But whenever she is helped towards divorce she backs down and there is a reconciliation. At these times she and her husband co-operate with social workers, rent collectors and the education welfare officers and make promises which stand for only a few weeks if they stand at all. The rent arrears are over a hundred pounds and there is a possession order in the hands of the Housing Department. The electricity has been cut off because of the long-standing debt. The Housing Department have recently been attempting to improve rent payment by evicting serious defaulters. They then rehouse them in sub-standard or unpopular accommodation, which tends to be high-rise flats. The Tenants' Association in the block to which they are likely to be moved has indicated to the Housing Department that they do not want this family because of the notorious behaviour of the older children.

The Social Services Department are involved in three ways with the family: social workers are involved with the children and the family over their general social problems, senior officers are involved in negotiating with the Housing Department to protect some families from eviction if the experience would seem to be too destructive to the family and there are also community workers who are involved in facilitating the activities of Tenants' Associations.

Comment

Although it is the anti-social behaviour of this family which gives rise to their immediate problems, there clearly are other problems in the family as well. The case notes do not make it clear what the Stephens' attitude was towards the delinquency of their children and their own failure to pay their bills. So we cannot tell whether their problems arise out of their non-acceptance of society's values or out of an inability to cope with their own personal problems. The social workers concerned have to decide whether their primary responsibility is to the other members of the community who believe they ought to be protected from behaviour such as that of the Stephens family, or whether they should concentrate on helping the Stephens to cope with their own immediate problems. Might one hope to do both things?

Case Three: the Walsh Family

Mrs Walsh and her six children live in a three-bedroomed council house. Mrs Walsh sleeps in one bedroom with the four youngest children. The two boys, one of whom is working, each have one of the other two bedrooms. Mr Walsh left the home three years ago and lives with another woman. He maintains contact with the children and keeps his new home in immaculate condition.

The Walsh home is chaotic, very dirty and overrun by three dogs and several cats, one of which has just produced a litter. There are regular complaints from neighbours and from the Housing Department about the general state of the house and garden. The children have very bad school attendance records: the 6-year-old has hardly made an attendance in his first school year in spite of the existence of supervision orders to the Social Services Department. The Health Inspector has recently been in the home because all the family have had infectious hepatitis. What is exceptional about this case of a multi-problem family is that the mother is an expansive, loving person and the children are friendly, outgoing and non-delinquent. In fact, the older boys operate their own 'intermediate treatment' scheme training them-selves and the dogs to catch rabbits on the marshes, and keep themselves out of mischief!

Mrs Walsh gains considerable support for her expansive

generous nature; her GP issues retrospective sick notes to cover the children's absence from school. She is a living commitment to the view that irresponsible generosity is a value to be held as more worthy of respect than responsible conformity and cleanliness. Social workers in the case have been pulled towards the mother's permissive view and have been very reluctant to enforce the supervision orders by authoritarian methods such as inviting the Juvenile Court to commit the children into care to ensure school attendance. They have, however, made less effect on the offensive dirtiness of the house than has the Health Inspector with his authoritarian approach.

An interesting aspect of family interaction is revealed by the eldest boy who keeps his own bedroom in first-class order, who was worth £8 per week to his mother when on Supplementary Benefit, but who is now working and pays £5 per week. He and his brother will not sacrifice their bedrooms and all the rest of the family are left in the only other bedroom. The family will not get a larger council house unless their rent payments are better, and the house is kept in good order. All non-authoritarian methods have failed to achieve these objectives.

Comment
One problem here concerns self-determination. If the social worker decides that because of his commitment to self-determination he must allow Mrs Walsh to continue her life-style, then the house will get dirtier, the children will not get a school education and the family may be evicted. If the social worker does not intervene then pressures from the community may enforce conformity in more destructive ways. This kind of case may involve a general problem for the principle of self-determination. An individual's actions will almost always affect those around him, so if he is allowed to be fully self-determining he may do serious harm to others. These problems are particularly severe when the actions of one member of a family seem harmful to other members. In such circumstances the social worker is almost bound to focus his attention on the family group rather than any particular individual. But it is not clear how the principle of self-determination would apply in such cases.

Other problems concern the interaction of the community. We may well think that Mrs Walsh's behaviour will damage the interests of her children and infringe the rights of her neighbours. But it is by no means clear what these interests and rights are. Our assessment of them will depend on the value-judgements which we bring to the situation.

Finally, it is worth noticing the way in which the case report describes the conflict between Mrs Walsh and the wider community. It suggests that there is a choice between 'irresponsible generosity' and 'responsible conformity'. You may want to ask whether these are the only alternatives or whether there is some other possibility – perhaps 'responsible generosity'. How would you proceed? How would you argue for your objectives?

Reading

1. On values and the description of need:
   Benn and Peters (1959), Ch. 6;
   Hare (1962), Ch. 7.

2. On anti-social behaviour and mental health:
   Clare (1976);
   Flew (1973);
   Szasz (1974).

3. On client–worker understanding:
   Rees (1978);
   Timms and Mayer (1970).

4. For further reading see the Notes in Part II on Mental Health and Mental Illness, Moral Harm, Non-Judgemental Attitude, Punishment, Responsibility, Self-determination, and Values.

4 The Concept of 'a Problem'

Introduction

We often have problems whose solution is difficult to see. And we may need to consult someone else, perhaps a professional, to help find a solution. Sometimes the problems themselves are difficult to see. We may be sure that *something* is wrong, but not sure just what it is. And of course sometimes we are quite sure what is wrong and are mistaken. In the vocabulary of the social work profession this fact is marked by the phrase 'the presenting problem'.

Social work has been described as a 'problem-solving' process, but it is difficult for social workers to help clients with their problems unless they can reach agreement about what those problems are. Sometimes the client may recognise that he has a problem but be unable to identify it. Sometimes the client may think he knows what the problem is but the social worker may believe that the client is mistaken, i.e. he may not accept the client's own description of his problem. There are also cases where the client simply does not recognise that there is any problem, although the social worker believes that there is.

There are many different reasons why a social worker may reject the client's description of the problem: he may be able to adopt a more detached and impartial view because he is not personally involved in the situation; his previous work experience may enable him to see points which the client misses; or he may see the case differently because he views it within the theoretical framework and the picture of social relations – psychoanalytic, behaviourist, Marxist, or whatever, which he acquired in training. But, of course, the social worker's judgement is fallible. He too may misidentify the problem. So there are two dangerous paths the social worker should avoid: uncritical acceptance of the client's view of the problem, and insensitive imposition of his own interpretation of the problem upon the client.

Whenever there is disagreement between the client and the professional in the description of 'the problem' a number of moral issues come to the fore. In discussion of the cases that follow, you may like to concentrate on issues related to two widely supported values in social work: client self-determination and being non-judgemental. Both values are usually asserted not in relation to a client's *description* of his difficulty, but in relation to his *actions*. To support client self-determination is to support the client in *doing* what he thinks appropriate; a non-judgemental approach requires some kind of tolerance of what the client *does* or has *done*. However, there is clearly a connection between a client's description of his difficulty and his actions, if he is active at all. What he *does* about his problem reflects his view of what is his problem. Particular activities are solutions to particular problems, not *any* problem. For example, swimming as a *solution* shows that you see your problem as 'being in danger of drowning', or 'being in danger of being eaten by a crocodile', or some other of a *limited* range of descriptions of your situation to which swimming might provide an answer.

Because there is this *conceptual* link between problem-solving activities and problem descriptions, commitment to client self-determination implies not only a degree of support for, or tolerance of, the client's actions, but also an agreement with his description of his difficulty. Given the difficulties often associated with the identification of problems in social work, discussed at the beginning of this introduction, should we modify our commitment to self-determination, and in what way?

Where the client's description of his difficulty itself implies value-judgements about himself or others, it seems that in either acceptance or rejection of his description, the social worker fails to maintain the recommended non-judgemental approach. For example, in the cases which follow the Kershaws and Mrs Downs describe their problems in a way which implies that they are good parents seeking the welfare of their children. The social workers' different descriptions imply a different judgement – that the parents are unconsciously maltreating their children. In the case of Ronald Macks the probation officer's different problem description implies a more favourable judgement of his client than does the client's own description.

Finally, we must remember the important part played by our values in determining what we see as problematic. Vegetarians don't find a meat shortage difficult to cope with. The case of Alice and Robert illustrates difficulties generated by the client's own social values.

Case One: the Kershaw Family

The Kershaws want assistance to build a WC and bathroom on the ground floor of their house, because their boy of 13 is suffering from a progressive illness which at present limits his ability to walk properly and will eventually make it difficult for him to get upstairs. There is one other child in the family, a girl of 14.

The boy attends ordinary day school and gets help from his school friends in moving around the school building.

Some help is available in the form of a central government grant through the local Environmental Health Department; this grant can be given only on the condition that it assists a member of the family to get access to essential facilities but it will only contribute £1600 and the adaptation will cost £5000. The Social Services Department has a very limited budget for adaptations and in order to assist the greatest number of applicants it urges the Kershaws to accept installation of a lift or stair-lift at a cost of £1500, as a suitable alternative to the desired scheme.

When the matter was discussed with the family by a social worker the parents rejected the idea of a stair-lift out of hand. The social worker asked why a stair-lift was unacceptable and was told that it would then be obvious to any visitors to the house that someone was handicapped. It became clear that every attempt was made to hide the boy's handicap and they spoke of the way they were losing friends because they did not feel able to invite them to their home, because they would see their son's handicap.

Comment

This case at first seems to be a straightforward request for a service to be provided by the local authority. However, it emerges that the parents' request for ground-floor facilities reflects a desire to install their son in the backroom and shut him off from visitors. What do you think is the parents' description of their problem? What is your description of their problem? Do you think their request should be supported? Should client self-determination not override professional judgement in this case? And in relation to client self-determination, are the parents the client?

This case also raises difficult questions about not being judgemental. Can the parents' request be supported without condoning their attitude? Would denying the request be judge-mental? There are certain standards of care we expect parents of a normally healthy child to achieve. If we cannot avoid being judgemental in this case, should we expect and accept less from the parents of a handicapped child, particularly when they feel capable of less?

Case Two: Ronald Macks

Ronald Macks was remanded by the Court to await sentence for an offence involving breaking into a warehouse with others and stealing a quantity of tobacco. He is 6 ft 2 ins tall, of muscular build, a failure academically, but verbally fluent and self-confident. He comes from the East End of London and lives in an elderly terraced house with a bright and competent wife and their 10-year-old son. The home atmosphere seems warm and friendly and the inside of the house is in a good state of repair. The neighbourhood is one where delinquency is not uncommon and there are several local pubs where the criminal fraternity can be found. Macks has not been in trouble with the police since he left the Army nine years ago. He has earned his living as a lorry driver and this had been for a vegetable wholesaler until about a year ago when he tried to start up his own business with two lorries from his previous employer. However, he had had difficulty getting the necessary licence for his own operation and, while waiting for it, has been forced to work for a local coal-merchant. This brought him what he regarded as a disgracefully low income.

Macks expects a 12-month sentence for the crime and has arranged for his parents to keep an eye on his wife while he is away in case she needs any help. He feels in no doubt about the criminality of his act – some neighbours he met in the pub suggested that he could act as their driver and he did so. The probation officer is required to produce a report for the court but there is no specification of just what the judge will regard as significant. Ronald Macks himself is not offering excuses so that he be allowed to escape the custodial sentence.

Comment
The probation officer can find many factors in Mr Macks's background which are common to local criminals: low school achievement and a culture in which criminality is not likely to lead to social disgrace are two, but the significance of these for him in this case is not that they may have led to this offence, but that they have not led to offences before. The important thing appears to be that this man achieved his sense of machismo for many years in a non-criminal way. It seems that the frustration of this man's previously successful life-style by bureaucrats who made him feel

small and inadequate had made him vulnerable to offers of anti-social activity: it was a way in which he could 'get his own back'. This was not *his* explanation, but he later indicated that he felt he had been 'understood'. The probation officer attached considerable importance to this in his report.

Mr Macks sees himself as self-determined, and his offence as an attempt to solve a purely financial problem. The probation officer's different description of his problem seems to leave more room for the sympathy which might help his client escape a custodial sentence. Are the two problem descriptions compatible? Does Mr Macks's view of his offence and the problem it was to solve make probation unsuitable for him?

Case Three: Mrs Downs

Mrs Downs, a widow and mother of a boy of 10 and a girl of 8, comes to an agency asking that arrangements be made to receive her son into care because of his bad behaviour. Caring for her boy is, she says, preventing her having a life of her own, and she also says that he is physically handicapped. A closer examination of the situation reveals her as 'creating' this invalidity: she demanded a taxi because he could not walk to school, but at school he happily played football. The time when she most happily cared for him was when he had a mild cold and she kept him wrapped up in a blanket on the sofa when he was fit enough to be out but she would not allow it. The boy seems aware of his mother's confusion of love and hate for him and he 'punishes' her by his bad behaviour.

Comment

Again we have what looks like a straightforward request for service that the boy be taken into care. If we consider Mrs Downs as the client then it might seem that to take him into care would be to respect her self-determination but it would also mean that the social services were condoning her attempts to avoid responsibility for the care of her son and endorsing her view of him as a burden, a view which is based on the apparently false claim that he is an invalid. It is more likely that a social worker would try to bring Mrs Downs to see her situation in a different way and to adopt a different attitude towards it. But then it might be claimed that he is imposing his judgement on the client. If we look on the boy as the client then it might seem best to take him into care in order to free him from the ambivalence and stigma of his present relationship with his mother. In that case it might appear that the social worker was endorsing Mrs Downs's view of the situation whereas, in fact, the decision would be based on the judgement that her view of the situation was wrong and bad for the boy. Should this be made clear to Mrs Downs and, if so, how?

Case Four: Alice and Robert

Alice (aged 17) and Robert A (aged 25) married in affluent middle-class circumstances. They had a daughter, Dora, then, two years later, a son, Sean. Mrs A had a private income from a family business. They owned their own house. Dora was settled in a private school. About four years ago, Mr A had to leave his stock-broking firm following a conviction for attempted fraud. He blamed his wife's high expectations for their debts. A year later Mrs A's income ceased when the family business was bankrupted. She blamed Mr A for their downfall: to a rented flat and state schools for their children. She believed (unreasonably) that he was unfaithful and began seriously to ill-treat Dora. Because of this Mrs A voluntarily entered a psychiatric hospital. Mr A looked after the children. Mrs A went from hospital to her parents and did not rejoin the family.

Dora, then 8, could not settle at the state school. She felt frightened of male teachers and said she was ashamed to have no mother. Mr A sought psychiatric advice about her truanting, obstinacy and insomnia. Sean (6) gave no overt trouble but was described by the school as a loner. Both children are highly intelligent and physically handsome. Psychiatric opinion was that Dora was depressed, reactive to her family's break-up.

Mr and Mrs A were divorced and custody of the children given to Mr A. He later took in a separated woman and her children, a situation Dora and Sean found difficult to cope with. Mr A later left the home, making no arrangements for Dora and Sean. His cohabitee appealed for help with their maintenance and care: she now had to work to support her own children.

Mrs A (now 27) married Gordon B (23). They sought custody of Dora and Sean, which Mr A was glad to surrender. Dora and Sean were looked after by maternal relatives, while the new custody issue was settled by the court. Neither the relatives nor the children were happy with this arrangement.

Since joining their mother and stepfather there have been many complaints of minor injuries to Dora and Sean. The actual injuries were not life-threatening, but there is well substantiated evidence (social work and psychiatric) of severe emotional abuse. It is clear that their mother has no appreciation of children's needs: she expects the children to forget their past experiences and start again in the materially comfortable environment she and Mr B offer. (She spent her own childhood in boarding schools.) She punishes very severely the most ordinary naughtiness and Mr B metes out physical chastisement after a warning.

Dora and Sean were taken into care. Mrs B, Mr A and Mr B all opposed the care order and threatened, with legal backing, to raise the matter again regularly. Long-term care arrangements are being considered. Dora and Sean are temporarily in a children's home where they expect a style of living foreign to the other resident children. The extended families of all three adults are trying to influence their view of where their allegiance should be: some of these relatives are previously unknown to the children. The children themselves are unclear whether their surname is A or B.

Comment

This family history illustrates the part played by social values in defining and creating 'social problems'.

Alice and Robert value affluence, so much that Robert will defraud to sustain it, and both he and Alice regard any contribution to its disappearance as blameworthy. When their expectations of continued affluence are dashed, each finds a way of holding the other responsible and the 'problem' contributes to the breakdown of their marriage.

Alice and Robert also value one particular manifestation of affluence, namely private education for their children. Only Dora is given private education but when this experience is disrupted, and the familiar experience withdrawn, her education becomes a 'problem' for her and her parents.

Again, Alice and Robert favour a certain style of living, presumably an affluent one, which Dora and Sean come to expect, and the absence of which will possibly make adjustment to the children's home later a 'problem'.

Dora and Sean are brought up in a society giving primary responsibility for a child's welfare to its biological family and giving children a primary obligation of allegiance to that family. When the biological family breaks up and forms other attachments, the new partners find their obligations, and the children their allegiance, problematic.

Is a social worker justified in attempting to solve problems of this type by changing the social values of his client? Is this approach compatible with commitment to client self-determination or to being non-judgemental?

Reading
1. General:
   Plant (1970), Ch. 2;
   Leighton (1972);
   Ragg (1977).

2. On self-determination:
   McDermott (1975);
   Mill (1859).

3. On the non-judgemental approach:
   Ramsey (1976);
   Stalley (1978).

4. For further reading see the Notes in Part II on Moral Harm, Non-judgemental Attitude, Self-determination, and Values.

5 Responsibility for Children

Introduction

In nearly all societies that have actually existed the major responsibility for the care and upbringing of children has been assigned to their parents. It is, of course, possible to imagine societies in which the state or some other social institution normally undertook this responsibility but such a society would be very different from our own. In addition to having the responsibility for caring for their children parents have also been allowed the right to decide the way in which their children should be brought up. In practice the rights and responsibilities often go together. We could imagine a society in which parents had unlimited rights to decide how their children were to be brought up but where some other institution had the responsibility for seeing that these decisions were carried out. We could also imagine a society in which parents had responsibilities but no rights – in such a society the state would lay down exactly how the child was to be brought up and would require the parents to see that they were brought up in that way. But in practice neither of these situations is likely to arise. A society in which parents had full rights but no responsibilities would be quite impractical because the state would have to provide the means for satisfying every whim of the parents about the upbringing of their children. A society in which parents had full responsibility but no rights would be impossibly irksome because it would leave parents with so little freedom.

Traditionally in Britain the rights and responsibilities of the parents have been subject to few limitations. It has been the duty of the parents to care for their children and no other agency would do this for them, but parents had complete discretion as to how they brought up their children. In recent times the state has limited parents' rights and has also taken over some of their responsibilities. For example, the state now provides free education and requires parents to ensure that their children attend school.

The social services are one of the main institutions through which society expresses its concern for children, but the rights and responsibilities of social workers can vary. All social workers have some responsibility for the welfare of their clients including children but this does not normally detract from the responsibility of parents, and the social worker usually has no right to determine what happens to children without the consent of their parents. But there are now legal mechanisms by which the rights and responsibilities of the social services can be extended while those of the parents are removed. In Britain these take the form of care and supervision orders. In the case of a care order the major responsibility for the care of the child and most rights to determine the manner of his upbringing are taken from the parents and placed with local authority social service departments. The cases in this section illustrate some of the kinds of problems that arise out of the interaction of parents and social workers.

Sometimes it is unclear who has the responsibility for looking after a particular part of the child's upbringing, or the parents may try to unload on to the social services a responsibility that is properly their own. So in the case of Jack one issue may be whether disciplining Jack is the responsibility of his parents or his headmaster. Both Mrs Atkins and Joanne's parents seem to want to unload some of their responsibilities (but not perhaps their rights) on to the social workers.

When the rights of parents are restricted the restrictions are governed by a strict legal framework. This legal framework often makes it impossible to intervene even when social workers judge it necessary. This seems to happen in the case of Mrs Atkins. In such cases there may be little that the social workers can do, but as citizens we may want to question the legal framework which allows this to happen or the decisions of the courts which act within this framework.

There are some grounds for supposing that children do best in a secure and stable family setting even though the behaviour of the parents may not be what the social workers would approve. So the social worker may have difficulty in deciding whether to support the authority of the parents or to weaken it by intervening. This is presumably one reason why Jack's headmaster encouraged his father to beat him.

Another range of problems is connected with the rights of children. Traditional practice allows children very few of the civil and human rights which are granted to adults; for example, children may be given very little personal freedom. Clearly many young children do not have enough understanding or reasoning power to exercise all the rights which adults have, but this does not mean that we can simply assume that anyone under some arbitrarily chosen age has no moral rights. So there is a problem about what rights children should be allowed to exercise. The case of Joanne may illustrate this. If she were an adult her behaviour would not be subject to any legal restriction even though most people would regard it as undesirable and immoral, but because she is only 14 attempts may be made to restrict her liberty quite severely.

Case One: Jack

Jack is 14. He is rejected by his stepmother but protected by his father who, nevertheless, is often driven to violent aggression towards Jack when his wife finds the boy difficult.

Jack arranged to go home from his residential school for the weekend. Instead of going home he went to the home of a school friend, Paul, some 40 miles away from his home. Jack was reported missing by his parents, who were very anxious and angry. On Sunday evening Jack returned to school with Paul. Paul's mother, who is a single parent, did not inform the school or anyone else of Jack's whereabouts.

The headmaster of the school took Jack home on the same Sunday evening to see his father and stepmother. Both were very angry with Jack and with Paul's mother. Father said he had threatened to belt Jack if he did this again. The headmaster suggested that he ought therefore to carry out his threat. This the father did after taking the boy into the kitchen; Jack returned in tears. Gradually, however, father and stepmother began to make positive, accepting statements to Jack, who then returned to school with the headmaster.

For the next two months Jack had good weekends at home, but then went off again to Paul's home one Friday night when he was expected home. Jack was found by the agency staff at Paul's home next morning. Jack's father was very angry with Paul's mother and wanted to confront her himself or bring in the police. The agency refused to give him Paul's address and Jack was collected by his father from the agency office in Paul's home town.

Comment

The case notes as they stand do not provide us with all the information we need to know for a full evaluation of this case. For example, we do not know whether Jack's attendance at the residential school was voluntary or compulsory, nor what the headmaster's motives were in encouraging Jack's father to beat him. He may have believed that those in authority should always keep their threats. Would you agree with this view?

From the information available it looks as though the responsibilities of the different persons involved were very unclear. In condoning Jack's father's action in beating Jack the headmaster was treating Jack's father as though he was responsible for supervising his son's behaviour. But the agency did not allow the father to take the kind of step that a responsible parent would normally take in this kind of case – he did not allow him to contact Paul's mother or the police. Do you think the headmaster's ideas about where his responsibilities ended and those of the parents began were confused? How would you define the roles more clearly in this kind of case?

One reason for refusing to divulge Paul's mother's address may have been that the staff of the agency believed that an encounter between Jack's father and Paul's mother would not produce the result he desired, but they may also have been influenced by considerations of client confidentiality. If this is so, then the case raises the question of the proper extent of client confidentiality. The staff of an ordinary school would probably be prepared to reveal the address of a parent to anyone who had a good reason for asking for it. Do you think these parents should have been treated differently?

A final point concerns self-determination. It seems to have been assumed that Jack had no right to decide how he spent his weekends. Do you agree with this? In other words, if you have a commitment to client self-determination does it extend to children?

Case Two: Joanne

Joanne is a 16-year-old girl in moral danger whose parents say 'we want nothing more to do with you since you will not do what we wish'. She has been placed in a residential hostel for teenagers but she wishes to visit the bright lights of the city every evening and sometimes does not return until the next day. The police sometimes apprehend her in the city and demand that the local authority accommodate her, she is accepted back at the hostel but such unconditional acceptance disturbs the pattern of the other girls who are regularly working and keeping reasonable hours. The girl's parents are constantly agitating via local councillors and complaining to the Director of Social Services saying that their daughter should be controlled, should not be allowed to be promiscuous and should learn that she must work for a living and act responsibly. The local authority can offer no other accommodation except a secure assessment unit or women's prison if they go to court and indicate that the girl's conduct is unruly (that she will not voluntarily accept restrictions on her freedom and that her conduct is a danger to herself or others.) They are also aware that should they take this course she will be in a position of living in an increasingly violent atmosphere in the company of more sophisticated criminal girls and exposed to more deviant sexual conduct with a homosexual rather than heterosexual emphasis.

Comment

One issue in this case concerns the idea that a young person needs to be put under some kind of restraint because she is 'in moral danger'. The very notion that Joanne was in moral danger involves a moral judgement which not everyone would accept. You may want to ask whether there is such a thing as moral danger and, if there is, how it is to be identified. But even if we do believe that Joanne was in danger of moral corruption it is not clear that she ought to be put under restraint because of it. She is old enough to understand what she is doing and we would not usually regard the fact that an adult was leading an immoral life as a reason for restraining him. It is not clear that a girl of Joanne's age ought to be treated any differently. It is worth asking whether the case would have been any different if Joanne had been male.

The parents in this case are obviously refusing to accept any responsibility for Joanne's behaviour and are trying to unload all responsibility onto the local authority. So far as one can judge from the case report the social workers have been prepared to go along with this. It is arguable that they should have refused to do this and should have concentrated on encouraging the parents to take their own responsibilities more seriously. What do you think?

Case Three: Mrs Atkins

Mrs Atkins is not yet 30; she was brought up in the care of a local authority because her mother abandoned her. Her emotional deprivation and her personality have combined to create an intelligent but demanding young woman who must have her needs met in any relationship before anything else can be considered. When she married she was pregnant by another man; there is now also a child of the marriage. The couple first came to the attention of social service workers when the mother was under stress from the demands of the second child who was then a few months old. Mrs Atkins phoned her husband at work and said she felt she was going to throttle the baby; he called the social worker who, on visiting, found signs of bruising on the infant's neck. The children were received into care at the parents' request and the mother was subsequently admitted to a psychiatric hospital as a voluntary patient. Two months later mother was back at home: the children were returned and the social worker visited regularly to give support and voluntary supervision of the care of the children. Day-care arrangements were made to provide an opportunity for regular surveillance of the children as well as relief to the mother. Mrs Atkins felt under much greater pressure from the second child; the first was exceptionally obedient, clean and docile, but the second provoked anger and jealous feelings in the mother. This is a classical situation for child abuse. The mother resisted the firm guidance of the social worker and started withdrawing the child from the day nursery; she also told the social worker not to call and was out when he arranged to visit.

The Social Services Department decided that the second child was sufficiently at risk that they should seek an order from the juvenile court to give them legal authority to supervise the child. They instituted care proceedings which required the psychiatrist, whose patient the mother was, to give evidence that she had recently suffered from some form of mental illness; it required the family's GP, who had given them immense support, to give evidence that they were in need of such supervision and could not properly care for the child without it. The GP was very uneasy about being critical of the mother's capability and he tended to forget or deny past incidents and was a weak prosecution witness. The case was clinched by the paediatrician who drew attention to the features of this case which were commonly associated with non-accidental injury. The juvenile court made a care order, although the Social Services Department would have been satisfied with a supervision order. They could, and did, place the children back in the care of the Atkins and continued to visit. The care order gave them the power to remove the children at any time if they felt it was warranted. The Atkins were very irate at the decision of the court and the GP supported them, as did their solicitor, in appealing against the court's decision. Although legal representation was under the legal aid scheme the parents were assessed to make a contribution towards the cost of the appeal. Five months later the appeal was upheld on the grounds that the court should only make decisions on the basis of evidence of conditions that applied at the time of the hearing and not upon the recent mental illness of the mother, from which she appeared to have recovered. The order was therefore ended and the family had a debt of £400 to the Law Society.

Two weeks after the hearing the Atkins asked for the children to be received into care and a few weeks later the parents separated and proceeded towards a divorce. The mother quickly formed a new association. The children began to settle down in care in a foster home and the mother maintained only irregular contact. Mrs Atkins then discovered that she had a medical problem which required her to have an hysterectomy so that there would never be the possibility of her fulfilling the role of becoming a 'proper' mother with any other children. She immediately asked for the discharge of the elder child from the care of the foster parents. The social services had no power to resist her claim; they could ask her to delay a little but the child was in voluntary care and the mother had custodial rights.

Comment

The law has confirmed that Mrs Atkins should have full parental rights over her children even though the social workers obviously doubt whether she is a suitable person to exercise those rights. So the case illustrates very well the conflicts that arise between the rights of parents to have custody of their children and responsibilities which have been laid on social workers to see that children are well cared for. From one point of view one might think that the outcome of this case is deplorable because Mrs Atkins was allowed to retain full control over her children even though the social workers who knew her best felt that they needed more supervision. The result was that there was no way in which Mrs Atkins could be prevented from taking her child away from its foster parents. From another point of view one might feel that the role of the social services in cases like this threatens individual liberty. If it were not for their successful appeal the Atkins' rights to bring up their children as they wished would have been taken away simply because a few supposed experts judged them unsuitable. One major question to consider is how, if at all, the tension between these two points of view can be resolved. The case may raise other problems as well. One of these might concern the grounds on which it is judged that people are unsuitable for exercising full parental rights. How is one to tell who is or is not an adequate parent? Another problem concerns the effect which the intervention of the social services can have on clients such as Mrs Atkins. It looks at least possible that this intervention may have made Mrs Atkins take her parental responsibilities less seriously than she would otherwise have done.

Reading

1. On our perception of children:
   Holt (1975);
   Hall (1972).

2. On confidentiality:
   BASW (1971).

3. For further reading see the Notes in Part II on Liberty, Moral Harm, Punishment, Responsibility, Rights, and Social Justice.

PART II

Notes

Introduction

We add here notes on a number of terms that have recurred in the case studies and in our comments upon them. The object of these notes is to give you access to debate of some of the philosophical puzzles associated with the use of these terms. We offer notes on

Liberty
Mental Health and Mental Illness
Moral Harm
Non-judgemental Attitude
Punishment
Responsibility
Rights
Role or Social Identity
Self-determination
Social Justice
Values

You may have experienced particular difficulty with other terms, of course. Try one of these sources:
Edwards (1967);
Flew (1979).

Liberty

One central question here is 'How far is the state, or any other organ of society, justified in interfering with the freedom of - individuals to do whatever they choose?' The most important discussion of this problem is in J. S. Mill, *On Liberty*. Mill's main principle is that society may interfere with what an individual does only in order to prevent him doing harm to others. This principle is generally taken to exclude two kinds of state interference:

(1) *Legal moralism*, i.e. intervention by the law to prevent people doing what is morally wrong even where the forbidden acts do no harm to others; for example, legislation which prohibits sadistic acts between consenting adults.
(2) *Legal paternalism*, i.e. laws designed to prevent people doing harm to themselves; for example, legislation requiring motor cyclists to wear crash helmets.

Mill's 'harm principle' has exercised immense influence and underlies much recent 'permissive' legislation. But there are some serious difficulties in it:

(1) Almost any action might affect other people in some way or other so it could be claimed that almost any kind of interference by society could be justified by reference to Mill's principle.
(2) Mill and his followers agree that his principle does not apply to people such as infants or the insane who are not capable of taking rational decisions. But then the problem arises 'How exactly do we tell who is and who is not capable of rational decision?'
(3) It is not clear whether offending someone is a kind of harm or whether there is such a thing as 'moral harm'. If we did count both of these as genuine cases of harm, then the state could exercise quite close control over people's moral behaviour without infringing Mill's principle.

Reading
Mill (1859) Ch. I;
Downie (1971) pp. 103–11;
Feinberg (1973) Chs. 1–3;
Benn and Peters (1959) Ch. 10, especially pp. 220–4;
McDermott (1975) Chs. 9–13;
Wolff (1968).

For the most important modern contributions to the discussion of these problems see
Hart (1963);
Devlin (1965).

Mental Health and Mental Illness
Although phrases like 'mental health' and 'mental illness' have been used for a very long time, the terms 'health' and 'illness' have their primary application to the body. A person is physically ill if some part or parts of his body are not functioning correctly. To call a person 'mentally ill' is, therefore, to suggest that his mind is somehow failing to function properly. The trouble is that the criteria to be used in deciding whether the mind functions correctly are not nearly so clear or obvious as those we use in assessing bodily functioning. A person is physically ill if the condition of his

body causes him pain or discomfort, if it is likely to cause his death, or if it prevents him carrying out normal activities when he chooses. Physical illness usually involves specific changes in the physiology of the body. The so-called mental illnesses, on the other hand, may exhibit none of these characteristics: they need not cause pain or discomfort, though they do often cause distress; they do not directly cause death and there need be no physiological symptoms. Some mental illnesses do not even interfere with the capacity of the sick person to carry out whatever activities he wishes; the trouble may be simply that he wishes to do abnormal or undesirable things. The mentally ill need not even feel unhappy; some of them may be unusually cheerful.

These points have led some psychiatrists and philosophers to question the whole concept of mental illness. They argue that society has used 'mentally ill' as a label for people whose behaviour it finds unusual or undesirable. By treating them as ill we deprive them of the respect and rights which we grant to other human beings; we allow ourselves to manipulate them by drugs and other therapies; in extreme cases we may even incarcerate them in mental institutions. The radical critics of psychiatry can point to cases where this kind of abuse has clearly occurred. Two notorious kinds of case are the categorisation of homosexuals as mentally ill and the practice of Soviet psychiatrists in regarding dissident political views as symptoms of mental illness. An extreme critic might go on to say that other psychiatric practices are not much better, and that calling someone 'mentally ill' is usually just a way of dressing up our own moral or political judgements as though they were facts of medical science.

In defence of psychiatry one may argue that the cases of the homosexuals and of the Soviet dissidents are extreme and unrepresentative. In the vast majority of cases both those who are called mentally ill and those around them are sure that something is wrong, they seek psychiatric assistance freely and, by means of it, are enabled to live much happier lives; to abolish psychiatry would be to leave enormous numbers of people in a quite unnecessary misery. If we accept this defence, as we probably should do, there is still an important lesson to be learned from the criticisms of psychiatry. It is clear that we should exercise the utmost caution before categorising someone as mentally ill. In particular, we need to guard against treating people as ill simply because we find their behaviour eccentric, disagreeable, or socially unacceptable.

Reading
Clare (1976);
Flew (1973);
Plant (1970), Ch. 3;
Skultans (1975);
Szasz (1974).

Moral Harm

Many things of different kinds are called 'harmful', from smoking tobacco to cream cakes, boxing and long-term stay in mental hospital. Often, a thing is called 'harmful' because of its effects upon our capacity or our opportunity to act as we choose. This gives us an important clue to understanding the term 'moral harm': moral harm is damage done to us as moral agents.

Thus, moral harm or injury is done to me when another person intervenes in my affairs preventing me from pursuing some morally legitimate purpose I wish to pursue. Similarly, moral harm is done to me when another person fails to keep a promise to act in a way on which I depend in order to fulfil my morally legitimate purposes. In these cases, and in cases in general in which my rights to pursue objectives which I morally may or must pursue are subverted, I suffer moral harm. Further, in so far as moral harm is less or more extensive, my status as a moral agent is restricted, damaged, or quite denied.

Any morality sets limits on what is morally permitted or required: killing fellow citizens is usually prohibited. On the account of moral harm outlined, this implies limits on what can be described as morally harmful. Having no right to commit murder, I have no such right which might be subverted, and thus cannot suffer moral harm in having such a purpose thwarted. Though, of course, like anyone else, would-be murderers can suffer moral harm by having those rights they do possess subverted by incarceration or whatever punishment is imposed, and, thereby, their status as moral agents threatened.

Special problems arise in relation to categories of people, like children and the mentally ill, who may have temporary limits set on their rights to pursue their objectives. What would be moral harm, a subversion of a particular exercise of moral agency, when done to an adult, may be described as rescuing a child from 'moral danger'. The explanation may lie in a view of the development of moral agency, and of education in its exercise. In the case of the mentally ill, some defence of temporary limits may be constructed upon a person's known objectives in periods of health. However, in respect of both groups there is much to unravel which is of particular interest to social workers.

Reading
Mayo (1978);
McDermott (1975);
Melden (1977);
Newson (1978);
Winch (1972b);
Jordan (1979).

Non-judgemental Attitude

According to most writers on the theory of social casework, the social worker should avoid 'judging' his client, i.e. it is not part of the social worker's role to categorise the client as a good or bad person or to assess his virtue or vice. This differentiates the modern caseworker from those old fashioned charity workers who saw it as their job to distinguish the deserving from the undeserving poor.

Although it is easy to see in a general way what is meant by this demand for a non-judgemental attitude it is not easy to give a clear or precise account of it. Writers on casework have recognised that the caseworker cannot avoid making some sort of assessment or judgement of the client's attitudes or behaviour. In many cases he can be seen as having a 'problem' only to the extent that his behaviour is somehow wrong or undesirable. It is sometimes suggested that the social worker may judge the client's behaviour but not the client himself. But in practice it looks as though we cannot draw such a sharp distinction between the person and his actions. Biestek suggests that being non-judgemental involves refraining from judging whether the client acted with knowledge and intent and is therefore responsible for what he has done. The difficulty with this is that a social worker who refrained from investigating whether the client had acted with knowledge or intent could not achieve any understanding at all of his client's behaviour.

It seems most likely that those who insist on a non-judgemental attitude in social workers really have in mind a number of different points. Among them are the following:

(1) So far as possible the social worker should avoid feeling anger or hostility towards his client.

(2) The social worker should not be dogmatic (should not have a closed mind) in making moral judgements.
(3) The social worker should try to see his client as an individual and not put him into moral categories, i.e. he should see him as the person John Smith rather than as a thief or alcoholic etc.
(4) The social worker should not be punitive in his approach. He should not try to arouse feelings of shame or guilt in the client.

Reading
Biestek (1961);
Ramsey (1976);
Stalley (1978);
Hollis (1967).

Punishment
When a word is used in a range of contexts, it is often, though not always, useful to try to identify recurring features of its use so that we can suggest what is 'a standard case' of its use. Other uses are then seen as extensions or as metaphorical. Philosophers have adopted this strategy for 'punishment'. Commonly, philosophers suggest the following description of 'a standard case' of punishment: it is unpleasant; it is inflicted on an offender, for an offence he has committed; it is imposed deliberately, it is not simply a natural consequence of a person's action (like a leg broken during an attempted escape), nor accidental (like the suffering of an over-ambitious jogger); it is imposed by an agent authorised by the system of rules against which the offence was committed. The punishment meted out by the state to a criminal is, on this account, a standard case, whereas the punishment meted out by Liverpool FC, at Anfield, is not.

Having identified a standard case of punishment and developed our understanding of the range of uses of the word, we may go on to consider questions of *justification*. Justification is essentially a moral matter, and justifications of a standard case of punishment generally fall into two camps: *retributivist* and *consequentialist*. All too briefly, the retributivist view is that punishment is morally justified as fitting, given that a moral offence has been committed: in the context of just law, punishment would be justified by reference to breaches of law. The consequentialist holds that punishment is justified if it produces the best consequences. It is not thought good in itself, but held to be admissible in so far as it promises, better than any alternative action, to exclude some greater evil. And it might do this, of course, by reforming the criminal, or by deterring him or others.

It is perhaps worth mentioning two areas of philosophical puzzlement of particular importance to social work. One is the relationship between punishment and responsibility. We usually adopt the principle that a man ought not to be punished for having done what he could not help doing. How are we to establish what he could not help doing? We may begin by distinguishing duress, ignorance of fact and, perhaps, irresistible impulse. The other area is the relationship between punishment and treatment. These are often implied to be mutually exclusive, though at times we also declare that 'punishment might be good treatment for a particular person in his particular circumstances'. It might be part of his moral education.

Reading
Flew (1969);
Hart (1968);
Hursthouse (1978), section 2.4;
Khin Zaw (1978);
Watson (1976).

Responsibility
The terms 'responsible' and 'responsibility' can be used in a number of different, though related, ways. The following list is by no means exhaustive:

(1) 'A responsibility' often means the same as 'a duty'. Thus it makes no difference whether we talk about the responsibility of parents to care for their children, or about their duty to do so. Similarly, it does not matter whether one talks of 'the professional responsibilities' or the 'professional duties' of a social worker. To say that someone accepts responsibility, e.g. for looking after his own affairs, is to say that he sees the duty of looking after these matters as falling on him and on no one else.

(2) A responsible person is one who takes his responsibilities (i.e. his duties) seriously. To treat someone as responsible is to treat him as one who can be relied on to carry out his duties without special supervision.

(3) In legal contexts a person is responsible for something which has happened if he is liable to be punished or to pay damages for it.

(4) In other contexts to say that someone is responsible for something which has happened is to say that he is the one who should be blamed or praised for it.

(5) Sometimes we say of a child, or of an adult suffering from mental disorder, that he lacks responsibility or has diminished responsibility. This means that he lacks the mental capacities that are needed if one is to be regarded as responsible in one of the other senses.

Although these senses of 'responsibility' are all different they are closely connected with one another. For example, a number of philosophers have argued that saying that someone has the responsibility (i.e. the duty) to do something implies that he will be held responsible (i.e. blameworthy) for not doing it. The different uses of 'responsible' and 'responsibility' can be seen as picking out different aspects of a single way of regarding ourselves and our fellow men. When we are dealing with adults who are not suffering from any serious mental handicap or disorder we characteristically regard them as having rights and duties; we expect them to fulfil their duties and we blame them if they do not. To treat someone in this way is to regard him as a responsible person.

Some strands of social work theory emphasise very strongly the need to see the client as a responsible individual. We are told, for example, that the client must, so far as possible, be encouraged to take responsibility for his own decisions and that enhancing his sense of personal responsibility can be an important part of the social work process. (See Self-determination.) 'Responsibility' is here being used in senses (1) and (2) above. There are, however, other strands within social work theory which tend to play down ideas of the client's responsibility. For example, the principle of the non-judgemental attitude requires social workers to avoid blaming or adopting a punitive attitude towards their clients. This implies that social workers should not be concerned with questions of responsibility in sense (4) where 'responsibility' involves 'blameworthiness'. The training of social workers in psychology and sociology may also lead them to be suspicious of ideas of responsibility. These disciplines emphasise that human acts have environmental or other causes. This has often seemed incompatible with the requirement that one cannot be held responsible (sense 4) for doing an act unless one has freely chosen to do it.

There is some tension between these two strands in social work theory. Some might even say that there is an outright inconsistency, i.e. that one cannot treat someone as responsible in sense (2) without also treating him as responsible for his acts in sense (4).

Reading
Downie (1971), pp. 55–7;
Benn and Peters (1959), pp. 196–210;
Hart (1968), Ch. 9.

Rights
It is important to distinguish legal rights and moral rights. There are two kinds of legal right.

(1) *Claim rights:* to say that someone has a legal right to something may mean that he has a claim to that thing which is enforceable by law. If I have made a contract to provide you with some kind of goods and then fail to deliver, you have a claim in law against me for those goods.

(2) The other kind of right is sometimes called a liberty. To say that I have a right of this kind to do something is merely to say that it is not illegal; I am legally free to do it if I wish. For example, I have a right to walk in the park.

There is an ancient doctrine that there can be no rights without duties. Two different points seem to be involved in this:

(1) If a person has a legally enforceable claim to something then there must be some person or institution which has a duty to see that he gets it. For example, if a social security claimant has a right to a certain sum of money as benefit then it must be the duty of the social security officials to give him that sum. Similarly, if I have a right to walk in the park then it is the duty of everyone else not to hinder me. In these cases rights and duties are simply different sides of the same coin.

(2) The other point is that our legal rights generally depend on our carrying out certain duties; for example, the social security claimant's right to benefit might be made void if he failed in his duty to tell the truth in making his claim. Similarly, my right to walk in the park depends on my carrying out my duty to behave in an orderly and peaceable manner.

Moral rights are sometimes rather like legal rights. In any social group there will be rules which are generally recognised even though they do not have the force of law. For example, there is a rule that we should tell the truth. We might therefore say that I have a right that you should tell me the truth meaning thereby that you have a moral duty to tell me the truth. This would be a moral claim right. We might also say that I have a right to wear fluorescent trousers meaning thereby that under the accepted rules other people have a duty not to hinder my wearing such things if I wish. This would be a moral liberty.

Sometimes it is suggested that there are rights which exist independently of any system of law or social rules. For example, it may be said that all people have a right to life and liberty. Such rights are generally called human rights although an increasing number of thinkers would argue that animals also have rights of this kind. If there are such rights then they are rather different from legal rights and the moral rights which depend on social rules. One important difference is that in the case of the so-called 'human' rights there may be no corresponding duties. A man on a desert island would presumably retain his human right to life but there would be no one who has the duty to give it to him.

In the context of this book 'rights' generally refers to legal rights or rights under conventional moral rules. There are two main ways in which such rights give rise to moral problems:

(1) There are conflicts of rights: one person's rights may conflict with those of another, for example, two different people may have legal or moral claims to the same thing. It may also happen that legal and moral rights do not correspond to one another; for example, I may have a good moral claim to something but not a good legal claim.

(2) It is often unclear what a particular person's moral rights are. The moral or conventional rules may be unclear in themselves; they may be in the process of change; or there may be differences in the rules recognised by different social groups.

Reading
Cannon (1975);
Downie (1971);
Feinberg (1973);
Melden (1975);
Walton (1975);
Watson (1980), Ch. 10.

Role or Social Identity

The word 'role' has been used in a large number of different ways. Sometimes it is used in such a general way as to be almost meaningless. There seem to be two senses which are important for our purpose.

(1) A role is often a cluster of rights and duties. For example, to say that someone has the role or job of a bus conductor is to say among other things, that he has a duty to ride on certain buses and to collect fares from passengers; he has a right to receive the fares from passengers and to receive wages from the bus company. The rights and duties in question may be legal or moral or both. Those who occupy the roles of husband and wife, for example, have both legal and moral rights and duties with regard to one another.

(2) A role is sometimes a pattern of behaviour which has come to be expected of a particular individual within a group. For example, someone may have the role of a buffoon or scapegoat. This means that he is expected to behave in a particular way towards others, and vice versa. Roles of this kind obviously play an important part in the dynamics of small groups.

These two senses of 'role' often shade into one another. The crucial distinction is between behaviour which is seen as a matter of duty and behaviour which is merely expected because people have become used to that sort of thing.

Reading
Benson (1976);
Downie (1971);
Loudfoot (1972);
Watson (1980), Part 1;
Winch (1972a).

Self-determination

The principle of client self-determination or self-direction has been central to the development of casework. The underlying idea is that so far as possible the client should be left free to make his own decisions and to choose his own way of life. The social worker must therefore avoid coercing his client; for example, he should not threaten him with punishment if he does not do what the social worker wishes. But it is not only open coercion which is forbidden by the principle of client self-determination. The social worker should also avoid persuading the client to do things that he does not really want to do.

The principle of client self-determination in the field of social work corresponds very closely to the principle of liberty in the field of politics and many of the same problems arise in the two cases. What, for example, should the social worker do about a client whose conduct threatens to do harm to others or to society at large? What should he do about a client whose decisions do not seem wholly rational? But there are also special problems about self-determination in social work. Many critics have argued that self-determination is in practice an illusion. By the very nature of their job social workers affect their client's behaviour. However much they may go through the motions of respecting the client's own decisions they do not and cannot avoid exercising a controlling influence over him. An even more radical criticism is possible. Many people believe that all human behaviour is caused by heredity and/or by environmental influences. This view is called *determinism*. It has been argued that, if determinism is true, none of our actions are really free and so the very idea that people can be self-determining is absurd.

Reading
Biestek (1961), Part 2, principle 6;
Hollis (1967);
Plant (1970), pp. 25–34;
McDermott (1975), Chs. 1–8, 15.

Social Justice
One way of looking at the problems of deprived clients is to say that they have been unjustly treated by society and deserve to be compensated for this. A good deal then depends on one's conception of social justice.

Most philosophers have agreed that justice consists in some form of equality but they have disagreed considerably as to what form of equality constitutes justice. Some possibilities are

(1) Absolute equality of wealth and/or income.
(2) Equal benefits for equal needs; i.e. those with the same needs should have equal shares of whatever is required to satisfy those needs.

(3) Equality of opportunity; i.e. everyone must be given an equal chance of competing in the race, though some will be more successful than others.
(4) Equal rewards for equal merit; 'merit' can here be defined in many different ways (e.g. intelligence, virtue, etc.).
(5) Equal rewards for equal effort.
(6) Equal rewards to those who have made equal contributions to society.

It may also be argued that other considerations sometimes justify us in overriding equality. For example, one may say that although it would be nice to give equal benefits to all men it is necessary to have some inequalities in order to give people an incentive to work hard and use their talents for the good of society. Similarly, it may be argued that a really equal society could not be free and so equality must sometimes be overridden in order to secure liberty.

In practice all these ideas play some part in most modern western thought about social justice. A good deal of political and social thought has been concerned with trying to integrate them into one consistent theory but there is no conception of social justice which would be accepted by all philosophers.

If one describes any part of the social worker's activity as rectifying injustice much will depend on what concept of justice one works with. Thus if we think primarily in terms of equal rewards for equal efforts we may feel little sympathy for a client who has made no serious attempt to look for a job. If we stress equality of need we may take a very different view.

Reading
Feinberg (1973), Ch. 7;
Benn and Peters (1959), Chs. 5 and 6;
George and Wilding (1976), Ch. 6;
Watson (1980), Part 2;
Weale (1978).

Values
Our values are the principles by which we decide what is good or bad and what we ought or ought not to do. They provide the standards by which we judge our own behaviour and that of others. We must be careful to distinguish values from mere preferences or likings. I may, for example, *prefer* whisky to gin but that does not necessarily mean that I think everyone ought to drink whisky. If,

on the other hand, I value a sober way of life then I will consider that this is the sort of life everyone ought to live.

Even when we have distinguished values from mere preferences the word 'value' may still be used to describe many different kinds of thing. At one extreme there are values to which almost all civilised people would attach great importance. For example, most of us value human life at least to the extent of disapproving of murder. This value may well be essential to any decent way of life. Then there are values which have played an important part in particular societies even though they are not accepted outside those societies. Thus many societies have placed a high value on noble birth while other societies have managed quite successfully without recognising this value. There are also values that are even less important or even more limited than these – values that are not taken terribly seriously or values that are confined to relatively small social groups.

Another distinction which can be made is that between social values and individual values. Social values concern our relation-ships with other people, they are shared by all or most members of a social group and those who accept the values usually think of them as binding on everybody, or at least on all members of the group. Thus the obligation to keep a promise is a social value. Individual values, on the other hand, may not be shared, they may concern the purely private part of our lives and we may not think of them as binding on other people. Thus we may set ourselves standards of sexual morality or of religious behaviour, for example, without thinking of them as binding on others.

Each person has his own value system which will be largely influenced by the social groups to which he belongs but will also show individual variations. An important part of respecting a person is taking his values seriously however trivial or alien they may seem to us.

A good deal of confusion has been caused by failing to distinguish between values and preferences and among different kinds of value. If one fails to make these distinctions one may be led to think them all arbitrary and unimportant. But clearly there are some values that are fundamental to social life and others that cannot be rejected wthout committing oneself to a wholesale social change.

The social worker's position is especially difficult because he has to take account, not only of his own values, but also of the values of his clients, of his profession and those of the wider society to which he belongs.

Reading
Downie (1971), Ch. 2;
Benn and Peters (1959), Ch. 2;
Strawson (1961).

References

BASW (1971), 'Confidentiality in Social Work', Discussion Paper no. 1, Birmingham, British Association of Social Workers

Benn, S. I. and Peters, R. S. (1959), *Social Principles and the Democratic State,* London, Allen & Unwin.

Benson, J. (1976), 'The Concept of Community', in N. Timms and D. Watson (eds.), *Talking about Welfare,* London, Routledge & Kegan Paul, 1976.

Biestek, F. (1961), *The Casework Relationship,* London, Allen & Unwin.

CCETSW (1976), 'Values in Social Work', Discussion Paper 13, London, Central Council for Education and Training in Social Work.

Cannan, C. (1975), 'Welfare Rights and Wrongs', in R. Bailey and M. Brake (eds.), *Radical Social Work,* London, Edward Arnold, 1975.

Clare, A. (1976), *Psychiatry in Dissent,* London, Tavistock.

Devlin, P. (1965), *The Enforcement of Morals,* Oxford, Oxford University Press.

Downie, R. S. (1971), *Roles and Values,* London, Methuen.

Edwards, P. (ed.) (1967), *The Encyclopedia of Philosophy,* New York, Macmillan.

Feinberg, J. (1973), *Social Philosophy,* Englewood Cliffs, New Jersey, Prentice-Hall.

Flew, A. (1969), 'The Justification of Punishment', in H. B. Acton (ed.), *The Philosophy of Punishment,* London, Macmillan, 1969.

Flew, A. (1973), *Crime or Disease?,* London, Macmillan.

Flew, A. (ed.) (1979), *A Dictionary of Philosophy,* London, Pan.

Foren, R. and Bailey, R. (1968), *Authority in Social Casework,* London, Pergamon.

Frankena, W. (1963), *Ethics,* Englewood Cliffs, New Jersey, Prentice-Hall.

George, V. and Wilding, P. (1976), *Ideology and Social Welfare,* London, Routledge & Kegan Paul.

Glennerster, H. and Hatch, S. (eds.) (1974), 'Positive Discrimination and Inequality', Fabian Research Series Pamphlet 314, London, Fabian Society.

Hall, J. (ed.) (1972), *Children's Rights,* London, Panther.

Hanfling, O. (1978), *Uses and Abuses of Argument,* Units 2B and 9 of A101, Arts Foundation Course, Milton Keynes, Open University Press.

Hare, R. M. (1962), *The Language of Morals,* Oxford, Clarendon Press.

Hart, H. L. A. (1963), *Law, Liberty and Morality,* Oxford, Oxford University Press.

Hart, H. L. A. (1968), *Punishment and Responsibility,* Oxford, Oxford University Press.

Hollis, F. (1967), 'Principles and Assumptions Underlying Casework Practice', in E. Younghusband (ed.), *Social Work and Social Values,* London, Allen & Unwin, 1967.

Holt, J. (1975), *Escape from Childhood,* Harmondsworth, Penguin.

Hospers, J. (1962), *Human Conduct,* London, Rupert Hart-Davis.

Hursthouse, R. (1978), *Introduction to Philosophy,* Arts Foundation Course Units 13, 14 and 15, Milton Keynes, Open University Press.

Jordan, W. (1979), *Helping in Social Work,* London, Routledge & Kegan Paul.

Khin Zaw, S. (1978), '"Irresistible Impulse" and Moral Responsibility', in G. N. A. Vesey (ed.), *Human Values,* Hassocks, Harvester Press, 1978.

Langford, G. (1972), *Human Action,* London, Macmillan.

Leighton, N. (1972), 'The Act of Understanding', *British Journal of Social Work,* Vol. 2, no. 4.

Lindley, R., Fellows, R. and Macdonald, G. (1978), *What Philosophy Does,* London, Open Books.

Loudfoot, E. (1972), 'The Concept of Social Role', *Philosophy of Social Science,* Vol. 2.

McDermott, F. (ed.) (1975), *Self-Determination in Social Work,* London, Routledge & Kegan Paul.

Mayo, B. (1978), 'Moral Integrity', in G. N. A. Vesey (ed.), *Human Values,* Hassocks, Harvester Press, 1978.

Melden, A. I. (1975), 'Rights and Right Conduct', in F. McDermott (ed.), *Self-Determination in Social Work,* London, Routledge & Kegan Paul, 1975.

Melden, A. I. (1977), *Rights and Persons,* Oxford, Blackwell.

Mill, J. S. (1859), 'On Liberty', reprinted in M. Warnock (ed.), *Utilitarianism, John Stuart Mill,* London, Collins, 1962.

Newson, E. (1978), 'Unreasonable Care: the establishment of selfhood', in G. N. A. Vesey (ed.), *Human Values,* Hassocks, Harvester Press, 1978.

O'Connor, D. J. (1972), *Free Will,* London, Macmillan.

Peters, R. S. (1958), *The Concept of Motivation,* London, Routledge & Kegan Paul.

Pinker, R. (1971), *Social Theory and Social Policy,* London, Heinemann.

Plant, R. (1970), *Social and Moral Theory in Casework,* London, Routledge & Kegan Paul.

Ragg, N. (1977), *People not Cases*, London, Routledge & Kegan Paul.

Ramsey, I. T. (1976), 'On Not Being Judgemental', in N. Timms and D. Watson (eds.), *Talking about Welfare,* London, Routledge & Kegan Paul, 1976.

Raphael, D. D. (1970), *Problems of Political Philosophy,* London, Macmillan.

Rees, S. (1978), *Face to Face with Social Work,* London, Edward Arnold.

Skultans, V. (1975), *Madness and Morals,* London, Routledge & Kegan Paul.

Stalley, R. F. (1978), 'Non-judgemental Attitudes', in N. Timms and D. Watson (eds.), *Philosophy in Social Work,* London, Routledge & Kegan Paul, 1978.

Strawson, P. F. (1961), 'Social Morality and the Individual Ideal', *Philosophy,* Vol. 36, no. 136.

Szasz, T. (1974), *Ideology and Insanity,* Harmondsworth, Penguin.

Timms, N. and Mayer, J. E. (1970), *The Client Speaks,* London, Routledge & Kegan Paul.

Titmuss, R. M. (1968), *Commitment to Welfare,* London, Allen & Unwin.

Walton, R. G. (1975), 'Welfare Rights and Social Work', in H. Jones (ed.), *Towards a New Social Work,* London, Routledge & Kegan Paul, 1975.

Warnock, G. J. (1967), *Contemporary Moral Philosophy,* London, Macmillan.

Watson, D. (1975), 'Freedom from Welfare', *Social Work Today,* Vol. 6, no. 8.

Watson, D. (1976), 'The Underlying Principles', in F. Martin and K. Murray (eds.), *Children's Hearings,* Edinburgh, Scottish Academic Press, 1976.

Watson, D. (1980), *Caring for Strangers,* London, Routledge & Kegan Paul.

Weale, A. (1978), *Equality and Social Policy,* London, Routledge & Kegan Paul.

Winch, P. (1972a), 'Nature and Convention', in P. Winch (ed.), *Ethics and Action,* London, Routledge & Kegan Paul, 1972.

Winch, P. (1972b), 'Moral Integrity', in P. Winch (ed.), *Ethics and Action,* London, Routledge & Kegan Paul, 1972.

Wolff, R. P. (1968), *The Poverty of Liberalism,* Boston, Beacon.

Wootton, B. (1960), 'The Image of the Social Worker', *British Journal of Sociology,* Vol. 11, no. 4.